She Knows: Once Bound But Now Redeemed To Become

She Knows: Once Bound But Now Redeemed To Become

Nia Robinson

She Knows: Once Bound But Now Redeemed To Become

Copyright © 2020 by Nia Robinson

Published by Nia Robinson

PRINTED IN THE UNITED STATES OF AMERICA

ISBN: 978-0-578-69101-5

The Holy Bible, English Standard Version (ESV) is adapted from the Revised Standard Version of the Bible, copyright Division of Christian Education of the National Council of the Churches of Christ in the U.S.A. All rights reserved.

Scriptures taken from the Holy Bible, New International Version®, NIV®. Copyright © 1973, 1978, 1984, 2011 by Biblica, Inc.™ Used by permission of Zondervan. All rights reserved worldwide. www.zondervan.com The "NIV" and "New International Version" are trademarks registered in the United States Patent and Trademark Office by Biblica, Inc.™

Scripture quotations marked "NKJV" are taken from the New King James Version. Copyright © 1982 by Thomas Nelson, Inc. Used by permission. All rights reserved. Bible text from the New King James Version® is not to be reproduced in copies or otherwise by any means except as permitted in writing by Thomas

The text of the *New American Standard Bible®* may be quoted and/or reprinted up to and inclusive of **one thousand (1,000) verses** *without express written permission of The Lockman Foundation*, providing the verses do not amount to **a complete book of the Bible** nor do the verses quoted account for **more than 50%** of the total work in which they are quoted.

Book Cover Design: Sophisticated Press LLC

CONTENTS

Foreword 7

Acknowledgments 8

Chapter 1 - I Remember 9

Chapter 2 - Bearing the weight 13

Chapter 3 - The Wilderness 15

Chapter 4 - Missing the Love 17

Chapter 5 - Missing the Love Continued,
Where Do the Wounds Go 20

Chapter 6 - New Creature 23

Chapter 7 - Instrument 27

Chapter 8 - New Creature Remains 29

Chapter 9 - Reintroduction 35

Chapter 10 - Conclusion: Becoming..39

About The Author..41

Foreword

When Nia told me she was writing a book and the title "She Knows: Once Bound But Now Redeemed To Become," I quickly became very interested. The word that came to mind as I read this book was transformation. In over 25 years of leadership, I have learned that a lot of Christians are bound and have not experienced real transformation.

Real transformation starts in your mind, not your behavior. You cannot change your character simply by changing your actions. Rather, you change your actions by changing your character. And it all begins with changing the way you think. That's why the Bible says, Do not conform to the ways of the world, "but be transformed by the renewing of your mind." (Romans 12:2)

What is the difference between conforming and transforming? To conform something is to change its outward appearance by fitting it into a mold. To transform something is to change its nature. Conforming has to do with behavior. Transforming has to do with character. Notice that conforming is something you do to yourself- you consciously try to fit in or become like everyone else. But transforming is something that God does to you. It is God's work in your life, renewing your mind by his grace, through his Word.

I am thankful for the transformation in Nia's life. She has gone from broken and bitter to brighter and better. From living with abandonment to living abundantly, from a conformer to a transformer. It's my prayer that as you read this book if you're bound, you'll be redeemed to become.

- Pastor Contrell Jenkins

ACKNOWLEDGMENTS

First, I want to acknowledge God. Surrendering my life completely to You has been the best decision I have ever made. I love you with all my soul, mind, body, and strength. I owe all that I have to you — and that is my promise. Thank you for calling me, and establishing me to be a mouthpiece for your Kingdom.

I acknowledge my parents Erica Montgomery and Tirel Robinson. Thank you all for birthing me. I know that without you two, I would not be even writing this. Through you all, God saw to give me life and I know that my future will only make you all proud.

My grandparents, Beverly Montgomery and Curtis Montgomery. Thank you all for showing the meaning of selflessness. I know that my genuine spirit has come from witnessing you all be so genuine to me. Words can't express how grateful I am. Grandmother, thank you for ensuring that I remain well - taken care of. I know that you desire the best for me, and the best is beginning to surface. Grandad, words can't express how thankful I am for you. You are my best friend — even when we were at odds. Thank you for showing me how a man is supposed to love me. I have the best grandad in the world.

CHAPTER 1 - I Remember

> "I praise You, for I am fearfully and wonderfully made. Wonderful are your works; my soul knows it very well."
>
> Psalm 139:14 ESV

Early on in life, the phrase: "On your mark, get set, go!" were music to my ears. I dominated the 400m race. I was a professional and dedicated runner. Running brought so much joy to my life. I always knew I would place well for upcoming state and regional competitions. I trained hard. I placed my heart, body, and soul into winning. But surely, growing up, I would come to terms with reality. I thought winning was all I'd be doing. I believed nothing could taint my path. But life sure taught me otherwise. I would have many wins and many loses in my life. As my years rolled in, I would develop a new perspective and a new way of living. I would grow up and face the true music of life. Like rubber against pavement, I took off...

"Nia let's go to the hair salon!" is one of the earliest memories I have of my mother. Her voice was always filled with excitement and an immediate rush to get to the salon. Growing up, my mom and I made appointments every two weeks to ensure that our hair was healthy and looking nice. After my salon appointments, my hair always looked rich, thick, and shiny. The press and curl style was my go-to look. One day in my favorite store: Claire's, an employee of the store stopped me in my tracks to compliment how lovely and bouncy my hair looked. That was one of the first times I was stunned that someone else could see my beauty.

Besides my luscious hair, my eyes and skin ran second and third on my top list. My eyes are a very special feature, they highlight my genetics. My big, chocolate colored eyes always melted the hearts of my parents. My big eyes resembled my father's and my chocolate hue my mother's. I was the split image of my mom and dad, sometimes it was difficult to tell who I looked most like. On the other hand, my skin was what my grandma called, "brown skin beauty." How was I not supposed to feel beautiful and honored? But yet, one classmate began to unravel my insecurities. One day I wholeheartedly opened up to one of my friends about a boy I liked. He was so handsome, but he was white. And I was not. My friend unapologetically said, "You are too dark for him." I wish I could share how that made me feel, but words just aren't enough. That day, I felt less than. Like my skin was an obstacle, I began to question it all. To add more fuel to the fire, I was tall, really tall. Taller than all my classmates. So what if I had a "model figure" and nice clothes. Thankfully, I knew deep down I was more than a pretty face.

More than beauty, I had the brains and the determination to be the best. Ever since my elementary years at a Christian school, my foundation in Christ was built. I excelled in school. I remember being able to read and write at an early age, and qualifying in our schools' spelling bee. I was also very keen and free in school plays.

As time went on, I began to succeed in other areas. I dipped my feet in many areas I enjoyed such as acting and modeling school. Quickly, I became comfortable in my own skin and if I would have leaned in closer, I could have sent my modeling photos to agents. I could have been Tyra Banks 2.0, but I picked up new hobbies and enjoyed them very much. I began playing instruments like the piano. Though it was one of my favorite hobbies, I gave that up for dancing. I loved dancing, it consumed all of my time and required all of my energy. My coaches expected our best foot forward, they pushed us to be our best, and even though I loved the experience, I began to develop this "perfectionist" side of me. I began to critique every inch and movement I made. Big or small, I could pin-point my wrongs rather than my rights. Today, I can look back and see how my hobbies made me who I am today. The good and the bad, and for that I am thankful. If it weren't for my love of trying new things, I would have never found my true love—track.

I was a track star, I dominated the 400m race. I had a hunger and thirst for track. Track practices became my refuge, track kept me healthy, and gave me fulfilling friendships. Most of all, it made my dad proud. You see, my dad was a football player in his early years and in between seasons, ran track—it was as if I was continuing in his footsteps. One summer, I even made the Junior Olympics in Boston! Expanding and learning upon my gifts and talents was eye opening. I was able to learn more about who I was. Little did I know, there was still so much more to learn.

Seeds

Knowing who I was in God's eyes would take years to understand. Though I knew what I was good at, I didn't understand my innate actions to fill the void within me. A void I still had no idea I had. My parents protected me from outside influences and they did well in doing so. What they didn't protect me from was the influence within the nucleus of my "home." As a child and adolescent I didn't understand, but now as an adult, I can clearly see the seeds planted within my heart. I was bound by a seed I did not water. The enemy knew the seed that would hurt me the most, and without a choice of my own, I had to reap the harvest and eventually uproot it forever. You see, even as a child, nothing could kill the calling upon me. Who I was meant to be only God could help me form.

Early on, before my conception and within my conception, there was a seed that was sown. There was a hurt far beyond my control. What the enemy used as a burden, God would use as a redemption of my life and the generations to come. The feeling of neglect was heavy, afterall, I was born out of wedlock. As a child, I did not understand why I felt the way I did it would take me years to discover the root of some of the issues I faced. Waking up to my mom every morning and with weekend visits from my dad was my normal. Friday through Sunday were daddy-daughter moments. Growing up, I lived with my mom, and I would see my dad on the weekend. To me, it was not a problem — it was normal.

Friday's were chill days, Saturday's we would go out on daddy-daughter dates. Sometimes we would go to museums or to the movie theater. On Sunday's we would go to church and then I'd return home. My mom on the other hand, handled doctors appointments, parent teacher conferences, helped me with my homework after school, took me to all of my school recitals and practices, and did everything in between. My mom was the definition of Supermom. My parents did everything to give me the most "normal" family experience, but I knew my situation was not normal. I remember desiring my mom and dad together during one of my many parent-teacher conferences in elementary school. My mom had scheduled my upcoming parent-teacher conference, according to her availability, and out of the desire of my heart I asked, "Will dad be able to attend the parent-teacher conference?" Her response pierced my heart with a simple and strong, "No." I personally knew my dad would not be able to attend due to his heavy work schedule, but deep down I wished the answer would be different.

I longed for my parents to be together. It wasn't enough to live with my mom and spend weekends with my dad. It's safe to say that I felt a more consistent, firm, and organic relationship with my mom—she was the one I lived with. She stood by my side when I was sick, she was there to catch my loose teeth, and she was the ear that listened when I had to speak. My dad was less consistent. His presence in my home was nonexistent. I received the nurture I needed at home by my mom, but where was the protection I needed from my dad? My dad is by far a good man. His leadership qualities have allowed him to obtain corporate positions that most black males struggle to obtain. But as a dad, his negligence caused me much trauma growing up. The seeds of neglect, abandonment, and rejection were planted at an early age in my life. It would take many years to uproot. In the meantime, I was hurt.

The many weekends and church services could never fill my longing to have my dad at home. For a long time, I felt a whole in my heart—I carried the weight of my pain. My immediate situation needed more than gifts and hymns. I needed something stronger, bigger, and far more powerful than my own might. I needed a God who could tear down the generational curses and hurt in my life. I needed to see the green in my own pasture. With time, I realized only God could fill the void in my heart. Only God could equip me with protection, love, and healing.

CHAPTER 2 - Bearing the weight

"When my spirit was overwhelmed within me, then You knew my path."

(Psalms 142:3 NASB)

Bearing the weight of my childhood experience was too heavy for me to handle. I understand now that two can experience the same situation, but it can have varying effects on each individual. In my case, the weight was too much to bear. Though I had my parents in my life, the circumstances were not ideal or normal. Their separation as a couple was the root of my pain. The enemy used my circumstances to induce feelings of abandonment, leaving me insecure within. The insecurities I faced were only part of the problem, but the additional aftermath I faced created further weight for me to bear. As I began to mature, I began to understand that as a child, I had not been nurtured correctly. Pieces of me were left void. The places of lack left me oblivious to future hindrances they would cause. For instance, I didn't learn how to articulate my hurt without feeling weak, which then left me lacking my self-worth. As I look back, I felt robbed. The basic foundation I needed to stand strong on my own two feet was never laid. I was left standing on wobbling ground, carrying a weight that was too much to bear.

In my adolescent years, I stood face to face with my painful reality. When I needed the protection of a father and the nurture of a mother under one roof… it was nowhere to be found. My upbringing was different. It wasn't ideal or what I wanted. I knew deep down that my family dynamic was best left untouched, but I wanted more. Sometimes, it felt like I wanted a family more than my parents did, and that hurt. Thankfully, my grandfather was beside me to guide me and love me in unmeasurable ways. My grandfather has been the closest person to me in my upbringing. Him and my grandmother have played significant roles in my life. They gave me a sense of hope, protection, and in essence, the notion of what a family should feel like. I know that without them I would not be the woman I am today. Their "old school" values and their abundant love has made me better, but most importantly, their love has held me up when the darkest places held me down.

God is so strategic with the people He places around us—with time, we find how valuable their kindness, support, and presence has impacted our lives. My grandfather has been by far the best thing that has happened to me. I believe God has blessed my grandfather with a long life to walk me through mine. Yet, believe it or not, I didn't always get along with my grandfather. His wisdom was beyond my years and I was already dealing with so much emotional pain. Though I honor and respect his "old school" values now, I didn't always. They were actually the cause of tension between us. His traditional views counteracted my "new school" ideas. Though I knew his love was undeniably forgiving, we bumped heads. But as we bumped heads, somehow, our hearts bumped closer. We began to respond to each other's love rather than our differences. And for that, I am eternally grateful. My grandfather is the best thing that has happened to me and I will cherish our relationship for the rest of my life—he is beyond the greatest grandfather to ever walk the Earth.

Even though my grandfather nurtured me, protected me, and helped me become who I am today… sometimes he added to the weight I could not bear any longer. From misunderstandings to emotional defeat, the spirit of abandonment weighed heavy on me. As a teenager, I just wanted to be happy and flourish. But my environment was not conducive to anything prosperous. There were many moments when harsh words cut deep and kind words were scarce. I was lost, depleted, and without hope. I was bearing so much weight, so much pain, and disappointment. I wasn't sure how much longer I could stand. Little did I know, this weight would only push me deeper into the wilderness.

CHAPTER 3 - The Wilderness

"Come to Me, all *you* who labor and are heavy laden, and I will give you rest."

(Matthew 11:28 NKJV)

Life's experiences are torments weighed heavily. My heart was torn—I wanted a whole family, one without any lack. As I began learning and growing, I battled with my self esteem. I felt too tall and too dark. The seeds of insecurity were growing. The overarching comments of my height and skin color were engraved in my mind and heart. I entered into a season of insecurity which I can now call the wilderness. I did not know who I was and whose I was. I was not sure when I would regain my peace, or happiness, I was in the wilderness figuring out my survival. The wilderness is described as an empty, or pathless area—indeed this is where I was. The land was dry, nothing around me—I was alone, frustrated, and empty.

In my teen years, the seed of abandonment flourished, I felt it more than ever. My communication with my dad ceased. I knew he was alive and dedicating his best efforts into his career, but I also knew that I needed him the most—in this wilderness. His absence was obvious and the questions were inevitable. "Have you heard from your dad?" were the constant questions I endured. "No I haven't." I was a broken record, my pain was impossible to ignore. As my dad's schedule cleared up, we returned to where we had left off, but it was too late—the pain was resounding through my veins. The wilderness hurt me, but shaped me. My hope now is that my past pain won't ruin or alter future friendships or relationships.

In my wilderness, I remember being angry, and upset. I was lost and needed direction. I needed a pat on the shoulder, and for someone to lift up my head and say, "Chin up." In retrospect, I can correlate my season of wilderness with the Israelites in the Bible who were oppressed by their Pharaoh. But by God's grace, they were carried out of their wilderness into the promised land. See, God has a "promise land" for us, and He desires to deliver us from our oppressor—whether it's fear, worry, or the feeling of neglect. Unfortunately, I was blinded by the wilderness, there was too much fog in between my pain and the promise.

At some point, it seemed as if things were going to get better. But you know how the saying goes… "Before things get better, they get worse." Even as my insecurities began to release their hold, a new shift began. Eventually, my mom no longer wanted to reside in Illinois. Without further thought—by mid-summer we moved to the West Coast, Arizona. My mom was excited for the opportunities ahead and in some way, so was I. Once I saw the new scenery in the West Coast, I was illuminated by all the beauty. The palm trees, the hot weather, and the houses were built differently than what I was accustomed to.

For the first few days, life seemed like heaven on earth. I came to believe that I would once live the same extraordinary life I was seeing, even if it meant leaving everything I once knew. Unfortunately, even with the "rich" feel of everything around me, hell was lurking in the midst of it all. To add more fuel to the fires, I can vividly remember my Dad angrily and with reason stating that he had not agreed with the move. It put many miles between us and that certainly did affect our relationship even more. Once again, my life was filled with discord, lack of communication, loneliness, and lack of support on behalf of both my parents. Surely, these seeds would follow me into my future, causing me to discover a new way of living. After a while, I left Arizona. I chose a path that would leave me lacking and hurting even more. I needed my dad but now I also needed my mom—this created an extension of my wilderness. Just like the Israelites, I knew there was a promised land and I had to cross over—so I did.

CHAPTER 4 - Missing the Love

"Love bears all things, believes all things, hopes all things, endures all things."

(1 Corinthians 13:7 NIV)

My whole being was yearning for a special kind of love and care. One that could fill the spaces of abandonment in my heart. For a long time, the enemy played with my mind and heart. The enemy kept me living in a cycle of discontent and void. I was trapped. I needed to be freed and released from the spirit of abandonment. I could not continue living this way. In my early years of becoming a lady, I felt alone. Although I had some guidance in how I should care for myself. I remember many sit downs and talks, but no actual example to follow. As time followed, I learned on my own to walk-the-talk. I was tired of unmet expectations and the feeling of abandonment. Within the pain, I would become the powerful woman I needed in my life. I would learn to keep my word and stand behind my actions. I would not settle for meaningless relationships that did not add unto my life. For far too long I had waited for others to fill my voids. I would fill them on my own at whatever cost.

As a young child, I remember the difficulty in speaking up for myself. Instead, I fell into the trap of staying silent in hopes that someone would love me. Deep within my soul, I yearned for a love so true that it would cover all my pain and make me new. I didn't know then, but what I was seeking for was an "Agape" love. A Greco-Christian term referring to love— the highest form of love. Unfortunately, my ignorance of true love kept me trapped in relationships, friendships, and situations that did not pertain to my destiny. Staying in these relationships and situations backtracked me. But in the midst of my self-sabotage, I felt comfort in any kind of love.

The enemy is on the hunt to kill and destroy. As God's creation from conception, we are the enemy's target. The enemy does not play fair, without fault of my own, life's circumstances had placed me in an easy space for the enemy to kill, destroy, and devour my life. As I sought to be loved, my eyes opened. And there it was.... I had my very first crush. He had all the qualities I thought were good. He was super cute, tall, and he played basketball—my favorite sport. Not only that, but we had mutual friends, and all of our friends had great things to say about him. As a young teen, I fell head over heels. He was perfect, or so I thought. Sooner than later, he became my first "relationship." A relationship I will never forget.

I remember bragging about this boy non stop to my friends. He was everything I thought I wanted. His texts brought so much happiness into my life. Most of the time, my cheeks ached from how much his texts made me blush. Like I said, I was head over heels. I was confident that he was the "one." Soon enough, I shared my feelings towards this boy to my mom. But within a blink of an eye, everything came crashing down. The boy I thought was perfect, was not. One night, as I patiently waited for a text from this boy, I received a text from a close friend that he was cheating. I didn't believe it. I was convinced that he was the one and perfect. He would never hurt me. So I ignored the text and never confronted him about it. I fell into the trap of staying silent in hopes that he would love me and he did! Clearly, he would never hurt me, he was the one. But as we all know, the truth always comes to light. The truth is, I didn't want to let go of the idea that someone did not love me enough to care for me. Though I had experienced this before in my upbringing, I thought this time it would be different. But it wasn't. Once again, I was left feeling abandoned. The spirit of abandonment followed me. It was painful to place so much trust and vision into a love that was not reciprocated like I wanted. More than ever, I felt vulnerable and weak. When would this pain go away? When would I become wiser and stronger to step out into freedom? Were questions that circled my mind.

Without a doubt, I would find myself in abandonment over and over again. It became second nature for others to mistreat me, but in reality, I was the one giving them permission to do so. I didn't respect myself, how could I expect others to treat me any better? Over time, I learned to treat myself how I wanted to be treated. My discovery came from many days and nights of relationship with God. Through Him, I learned my value and importance in setting standards. Today, I can confidently say that I will not compromise my worth. My hope is in God. And ultimately, only He can give me the love I have so desired. In the beginning stages of my pursuit for God, I began to learn the true definition of love and I realized I didn't want any other type of love. Manipulation and lies were not love related. God did not intend any relationship to endure those hardships. Therefore, I would not pursue any love that wasn't one resembling God's. I was missing the love of the Father. And thankfully, I had found it. Today, my prayer for you is that you will experience the love of God, so that you may be able to tell the difference between God's ordained love versus the counterfeit love. I found my missing love when I stopped settling for less, when my relationship with God became sincere and when I began to see my worth in the eyes of God. Only then, will you be able to experience such love as well.

CHAPTER 5 - Missing the Love Continued, Where Do the Wounds Go....

"Let all that you do be done with love."

(1 Corinthians 16:14 NKJV)

I wanted to skip over writing this section of my life. Sometimes, being vulnerable hurts. I knew that this would be a great thing to add as it would put emphasis on "daddy wounds" but revealing so much is scary. Thankfully, I understand that relating to you and helping you is the reason behind this book. Therefore, allow me as I begin to unravel a little more.

As you may already know, at a young age we are oblivious to love or the responsibility within a relationship. Therefore, "young flings" are customary. What is not or should not be customary is allowing others to take advantage of us. As a woman, it is important to seek after someone who will treat you with respect, someone who will uphold your standards. Remember, if you don't have any standards in place, you will get taken advantage of. Set standards high, don't be ashamed of how you deserve to be treated. Waiting on "the one" who loves you like God loves the church is better than settling for just another fling. As I got older, I began to discern what a man truly should resemble. I was learning to see through God's perspective rather than receive the distraction of the men Satan sent my way.

Wounds improperly healed can cause much damage. For instance, I believe wounds can lead to isolation from others. This can leave them feeling lonely and vulnerable when situations arise. While other wounds can cause us to seek care from people who truly do not care for us. In either cases, we are open to being taken advantage of. Due to my naivety, I chased for others to care for me... which was a huge waste of time and left me hurting even more than before. See, I grew up "old school" and from that, I had an "old soul." It was customary to love everyone and always take their word as "gospel." But with an infected wound… that was not always or at all, my best course of action. After many learning experiences, I have learned to set boundaries with everyone, especially with those I love most. Setting boundaries can help avoid any personal drainage. Prior to boundaries, I overextended myself and was always left drained. With boys, it was no different. I never saw a healthy matrimony or received the "daddy-daughter love" growing up.

In romantic relationships, I would go in wholeheartedly and fall. I was weak. My wounds left me empty handed. I gave so much and received so little. Instead of relationships, I believe now I was in "situationships." As long as I had male attention—even when I did desire for it to be a serious relationship, I'd compromise my standards which left me watering those seeds within me without even knowing. I wish I could say I learned my lesson the first time, but this scenario played over and over again in my life. Eventually though, my pain was my greatest teacher. Most importantly, I allowed the power of God to break hidden ties I once had with people, He also renewed my mind and helped me become the daughter of God I truly am. Soon, I know I'd be on the mountain rather than in the valley. My promised land was near.

Part 2

In life, it is inevitable to experience some type of pain, hurt, or disaster. However, within our surrender to God, and Christ as the mediator, we can peacefully come to terms that our future and our peace is in God's hands. God can use our darkest moments and deepest seeds to showcase the plans He has always had for us. Let's cross over….

CHAPTER 6 - New Creature

"Therefore, if anyone is in Christ, the new creation has come:
The old has gone, the new is here."

(2 Corinthians 5:17 NIV)

In brokenness, there is a chance for pieces to be put back together. One day, while I was on a break during my internship schedule in high school, I recalled making a list of inner issues that I knew were not from God. I wanted to work on being a better me, and God led me to this moment of self-reflecting. I noticed my weaknesses or flaws all stemmed from the spirit of abandonment. I was honest with myself and wrote out many words, but here are some: insecure, bitter, and naïve. Though I may have been in that place, I knew God intended much greater and better for me. Deep down, I knew God would put me back together again. I'm not sure whether he'd use tape, glue, or nails but I knew he would not leave me broken and forsaken. With God beside me, I knew I could reach wholeness instead of brokeness. Life is full of different seasons. One day, my wilderness, my brokenness, and my desperation for a savior would lead me to a season I had never experienced with God.

One summer night in 2017, I stood face to face with my next steps for a better relationship with God. It all started with my attendance to a youth Bible study, I was hungry for more of God, but most importantly I wanted to surrender my all to Him. In my soul, I felt the need to snatch back what the enemy had stolen from me. I needed my brokenness—whole again and only God could do that in me. In those moments of intimately seeking the face of God, I could see my life in that of the woman with the issue of blood in the Bible. She was willing to press toward Jesus to get her healing. And healing was all I wanted. I knew only Jesus could restore me. I needed a fresh encounter with God, this only could make me brand new. Only God could bring me out of darkness, and into having an abundant life.

At first, what I thought would be an easy exchange became a sort of tug-a-war with God. My pursuit of God was evident, but the pressures of the world weighed heavily upon me. I wanted a new life in Christ but I was also a young girl in the world. I had to make a choice. If I wanted God to take full control, then I would have to step out of my own brokenness. I would have to step into God's standards rather than the world's norms. This tug-a-war was a fight. But God fought harder for me. He ordered my steps to confidently live for Him, even if the atmosphere was not conducive. There was the hand of God, ordering my steps to be confident in living for Him in an atmosphere where it was not so common.

My walk with God became clearer and it brought so much peace within my soul. I was living in the present healing of my past burdens. Finally, I felt free and light enough to pursue God rather than run to friends or social media for guidance. God became my friend and my only source of hope. I am reminded of 2 Corinthians 5:17 which reads, "Therefore, if anyone is in Christ, the new creation has come: the old has gone, the new is here" (NIV). My brokenness was gone and my new me was here. My new me began to learn the importance of living unashamed and freely as a new creation. I stepped into a new confidence—I had rarely known. In everything I did, Jesus became the center of it all. And because my vision was on Him, everything else flourished. I developed a new heart and mindset for everything I did and for everyone I encountered. Below are a few areas in my life that received renewal.

Language

During the course of renewal, my language changed. I turned my back on foul, negative language, and complimented my words with who I was truly becoming—a child of God. I was indebted with God for the fullness of peace and freedom that I wanted to honor him with all of me, and that included my words. The best part about God's grace is that it can be magnified for others to learn from. I knew the changes in my life would help others in the same journey. I wanted to be a light even with my words. I desired to carry myself with a gentle and quiet spirit, rather than appear aggressive and mis-mannered. Thankfully, through my relationship with God, I knew I was on the right path to being exactly who He had called me to be.

Being mindful of decisions

God has created you and me for a unique purpose. It is important to keep our mind steadfast on the vision of God. Through constant and prayerful relationship with God, we are able to see how our gifts and talents can be put to use for the Kingdom of God. For instance, I made a decision to write this book. God placed the passion and vision deep in my heart but it doesn't just take vision to proceed with the plans of God, it also takes our will to take a first step forward. I could have not written this book or postponed it. But instead, I decided that I was going to remain faithful to the vision that was put down on the inside of me, so that God could be lifted up, and that others would be inspired and transformed. If that's you today, I encourage you to take a step forward in the plans of God.

Clothing

How you present yourself matters. It's how we land our jobs and even dates. As I continue learning who I was created to be by God, I took more caution in how and who I presented myself to be. I believe how we speak, think, and dress is a reflection of our divine design. In my case, though I was now whole, I did not want to present myself as a woman in need of attention and validation from the world. Most importantly, I did not want to encourage that predicament unto other women. I wanted to be a clear and positive reflection of God's grace and love.

In obedience to God's word and for the love that I have for Him, I have chosen to cover up any revealing areas. As a woman of God, I much rather showcase my inner beauty rather than the outer. Outer beauty changes with time, but inner beauty can last a lifetime. I am so thankful God opened my eyes to a new way of dressing, one that is honoring to Him. In this new way of living, I have felt the shackles of my past broken by the immense love and support from God, that is a feeling I cannot and will not ever take for granted. My life as a new creation has come with many changes but many responsibilities as well. I knew once I became faithful to God's word, I would become an instrument in the Kingdom. Becoming a minister was never a thought or a prophecy spoken over me, but after a while, I knew that God had ransomed me and was calling me to a life of complete surrender to Him. My ability to hear and know of His plans over my life were clear—indeed, I was a new creature.

CHAPTER 7 - Instrument

"For we are his workmanship, created in Christ Jesus for good works, which God prepared beforehand, that we should walk in them."

(Ephesians 2:10 ESV)

In the context of music, an instrument is used by someone for personal, or collective use—to provide musical sound. In my case, being an instrument would require me to bring God's voice into the Earth. In Acts 2, God declares that His spirit would fall upon all flesh to minister. Through my relationship with God, I came to realize that my time to minister was now. This broken, but now whole, bound but now set free, lost but now on fire for God, girl, could and would become an instrument for Jesus.

Before I was even aware of the extent of my calling, I was simply passionate to help those around me. In the middle of my schoolwork or instead of resting, I would become a "prayer warrior" for others in need. One day, a teacher of mine shared that I brought such a "light" to the classroom. I took that opportunity and ministered to that teacher. In the most random, but most needed moments, spreading Jesus was, and still is my desire. I was content with being a light even if no one else noticed. My purpose was to shine light to others not attention. As I began digging deeper for God, I spent hours in my prayer closet. It became clear to me that my obedience was leading me to God's plan for me. Plans he hadinstilled in me within my mother's womb. The best part was that I was willing to take on that mission to serve Him in every and anyway possible.

There is a character in the Bible that received a word directly from God that launched him into being an instrument: Jeremiah 1:4-5 states, "Before I formed you in the womb I knew you, before you were born I set you apart; I appointed you as a prophet to the nations." God created every man and woman with a plan, this text clearly shows God's plan with Jeremiah and with us. Before we can fully live in the plans of God, we must understand that we are able and worthy of such plans. Our hearts and minds must be in the right place in order to make those plans prosper. Thankfully, just as God had revealed his plans to Jeremiah, God revealed his plan for me. God began doing a great work in me and placed me in positions of authority and prayer. More than ever, I felt his mantle over me. Guiding me and protecting me to do His work. Little by little, I began to see the importance of my voice. He took me from working in the background to taking bold steps in front of others. Shortly after realizing His plans for my life, I began opening church service in prayer and interceding in prayer for others. His hand was upon me and I knew this was the beginning of my forever.

One day in prayer, God began to speak to me, and He said to write sermons. Without hesitation, I began to write a sermon based on a passage I had finished reading, and soon I had written a few more. I never knew what day I would preach these, but I knew that God was preparing me privately, before He would expose me in public. On December 2019, I announced my call to preach the Gospel. Since then, I've been inspiring young women and using what I know of God to shine light into dark places. Being an instrument for God is what I desire to do for the rest of my life, unashamedly, and with confidence. The enemy sowed seeds in my life to divert the gifting and calling on the inside of me. But by the grace of God, I am no longer a slave to sin or a puppet for the enemy. I am chosen and walk confidently in God's plans.

CHAPTER 8 - New Creature Remains

> "Therefore, my beloved brothers, be ye steadfast, immovable, always abounding in the work of the Lord, knowing that in the Lord your labor is not in vain."
>
> (1 Corinthians 15:58 ESV)

Routine can lose its gloss. Every beginning is strong and passionate, but can we invest that same intensity long term? I have noticed the effects of beginning and neglecting certain routines. For instance, I have picked up many passions, such as special skin routines, hair care, and most recently makeup strategies. I am diligent in maintaining the routine until I begin to see results. As soon as my skin is clearer or my hair is shinier and healthier, I put an end to the routine. Until I begin to see the signs of blemishes and coarseness all over again. Nevertheless, routines also become tiresome and simply boring. Sometimes, similar routines with God may also suffer a halt based on how we may feel or how the situation may seem. Thankfully, God does not change with us or our situation.

As I kept dwelling in the presence of God and in relationship with him, I realized the importance of developing my identity in Him. My relationship with God brought so much peace, healing, direction and closeness. I wanted to go "deeper" with God, I knew there was still so much to learn and share with others. Even though learning and growing in God required more time with him, I was willing to sow into His promises for me. I was determined to seek the face of God and never succumb to the pressures of the world. I knew the fruit of my labor would flourish, there was no reason to stop the process. Though the enemy would have loved to see me give up and stumble within the seed of abandonment, God was greater. God held me close and protected me against the lies of the enemy.

Singleness

Based on what I know God to be, I am fully convinced that "casual dating" is not on His agenda for His sons and daughters. God is a purposeful God, in the Bible all marriages had a special purpose. A God ordained marriage is specially designed for a kingdom purpose. And as a kingdom daughter, I am personally waiting patiently for my kingdom partner. I am confident God is saving the best for me, someone who can complete our kingdom assignment together. Looking at the relationship of Adam and Eve, Eve was Adam's purpose mate and together they became one flesh. Genesis 2:24 states, Adam and his wife were both naked, and they felt no shame. God brought Adam and Eve together without the process of dating, which was very unique. As we can see, God makes no mistakes. Adam and Eve were meant to be.

Walking in singleness and waiting patiently for God to provide my kingdom partner has sometimes been difficult. The enemy has tried to throw me off course, by having people speak against me and my decision. In moments of testing, I remain strong and stand firm on my beliefs. Sometimes I have fallen into fear and discontentment in my season of waiting, but I always turn my eyes towards God's plan. I will not let the enemy have a hold of me, I will not fall into sin and go against everything God has already promised me. Through the strength of God, and being graced with discipline, I hold true to being pure, and waiting on who God has for me.

Loneliness

Romans 12:2 says, "Do not conform to the patterns of this world but be transformed by the renewing of your mind. Then you will be able to test and approve what God's will is–His good, pleasing and perfect will" (NIV). According to this scripture, it is a command to not conform to the patterns of the world. As believers don't conform, only then will we be able to discern and walk through God's perfect will.

When I began to experience God in a deeper way, I knew I rather live for God than in a sin cycle. I didn't want to live in a world of confusion and consequence. I wanted to experience all that God had to offer–His peace and reward. Although living for Christ has been the best decision I have ever made, it does get lonely sometimes. Especially when everyone around me is not living for Christ and instead living by the norms of the world. As a young adult, I have had to choose wisdom rather than momentarily fun. I remember my senior year of high school, I felt so out of place. I remembered being around so much chaos. Even in the midst of so many people, the experiences I faced daily would only make me feel more out of place. I felt pushed out or left behind by many groups of friends. Honestly, I would feel crushed on the inside. I was surrounded by so much, but yet none of my surroundings related to the path that I was on. Being young has its perks, but in this particular instance, it did not feel that way. Growing up, I was always a part of the "popular" group, I never felt on the "outskirts" of events or gatherings. I had an easy way of relating to others. I wore the latest fashions, stayed up on current events, and socializing was a natural breeze. I abided by the norms of culture. Soon I realized that my faith and inner choices would leave me feeling stranded by my friends.

I remember talking to one of my teachers, who honestly became a mentor, and simply venting about my experiences of feeling different. In the midst of venting, I received encouragement to continue to be me, and continue praying. Being able to confide in someone was great, and helped me, but the ongoing pressures of knowing that I was different never ended. Being different was not only my narrative in the school area, but because I was different in school, the sense of feeling out of place amongst peers transferred to when I would be at home. I did not need to party, drink, or be around people and environments that did not match up with my destiny. So, in my moments of feeling that I had no one to relate to, I would often find myself at home. I unknowingly began isolating myself. In the moments of being at home, social media became my everything. Through social media, I followed my friends and saw everything they were up to and I was not. I would see the wild excursions, parties, and "link ups" that I knew I would not fit in. Even though I knew I did not fit in, it was the lack of being around people that would cause me to feel discouraged in pursuing God. Since God was growing me, I had to let "dead" things go, and be ok with not fitting in any longer. Being discouraged, I would often question why it seemed to be that everyone else could go out and have fun, but I could not. Then after a while of questioning, it became clear to me that I had to identify what "fun" was and understand that living for God is the true definition of "living my best life."

Instead of questioning, and murmuring around, I had to cling to God, because He chose me to go through this season. I had to understand that there can be a sense of loneliness, but not necessarily being alone. Since God is always with me, I can never be alone. I began to understand that being alone is not bad, but whether I saw it as bad or not, would depict if I considered myself lonely. It is the enemy's plan to govern the minds of people. Do not allow the enemy to lure you into lies. You are not alone, God is with you. Being alone represents the facts of being by oneself, but loneliness is a mindset that is backed by sadness because of the isolation. So, there is a decision in my mind that I had to make. I was either going to understand that I was alone, but never lonely, or I was going to let loneliness enter my life and cause me to detour from this sacred time, and placement that God had me in.

I believe loneliness may be a factor into why people turn from pursuing God. It may not seem "cool" and because it is not "cool" not many people are participating in it. Knowing that a lot of people are not participating, and that your circle may be smaller, may cause sadness to follow being alone. Because of loneliness, the desire of being around people, may cause someone to compromise their standards to be under the comfort of men instead of God. In my alone season, which I may still be in, as I am single, I cling to God. He is my best friend, I can tell him everything and he will not complain or gossip about me. Instead of complaining about my aloneness, I have learned to thank God for standing by my side even when it may seem lonely. I have the opportunity to run to the God who makes the impossible possible, has all knowledge and wisdom, and that will remain the same God forever. With this in perspective, I am able to fully enjoy my season. When the time comes, I know God will bless me with like minded friends and we will be able to pour into one another with God's love.

Criticism

Criticism is bound to happen to anyone. Whether doing good or bad, someone is going to be in opposition of a person. In my case, even while doing good, I still had critics. I believe one of the enemy's tactics is to place critics in your path. When critics talk, discouragement follows. When people are against you, their talk gets louder and we miss God's voice. That's why it is so important who you surround yourself with. In my season of transformation, I suddenly became bold about God. I didn't care what others thought or said about me, I knew who God was for me and that was enough. I remember close friends noticing my changes and complaining that our relationship was no longer the same. Although it hurt to see the change in my relationships, I knew God was building me to who I was supposed to be.

I never wanted to seem stuck up or as if I was better than a bag of chips. I simply wanted to live for Jesus. I can imagine how that may have made me seem weird but I was not going to compromise my belief and relationship with God. Unfortunately, as bold as I may have seemed, the criticism of others hurt. People began to talk negatively about me, questioning my faith and who I was becoming. The enemy wanted to distract me and "throw me off my square." Thankfully, I had safe places, my mentors, who comforted me in this time. I remember saying to one of them, after being so discouraged, "But I know I'm doing right", and she kindly said to remain faithful, and not to faint in doing good. In these moments, I held on to 1 Peter 2:22 which says, "He committed no sin, neither was deceit found in his mouth" (ESV).

Just like Jesus held his ground and did not let the criticism of others hinder His truth, so would I. Jesus was obedient to His calling, I too needed to remain faithful without seeking revenge. Through my gentle and quiet spirit, God's purpose would come to pass. I believe people's words, before anything else, can get to me. As I stated before, I was the tall girl, and my beautiful brown skin was too dark for some boys. When critics come, I have learned to embrace their words, instead of letting them ruin me—after all being criticized for my model figure, melanin, and solid relationship with God are not bad things to be criticized for. I had made up in my mind that I was going to remain the new creature. There are some things that go along with that, though. So, in these moments of acknowledging God in my every aspect, there are attacks that come with—discontentment, fear, or loneliness. To resist falling into these places, I had to hold on to God's word and prayer. I persistently pray that I will not fall into the tactics of the enemy, and that anything that is thrown my way will be defeated. It is my consistent prayer that I will not be persuaded by the world, and the knowledge of the world. It is my prayer that I stay in the will of God and overcome temptation. I pray this may be your prayer as well.

CHAPTER 9 - Reintroduction

"But you are a chosen people, a royal priesthood, a holy nation, God's special possession, that you may declare the praises of him who called you out of darkness into his wonderful light."

(1 Peter 2:9 NIV)

In the midst of being redeemed by God, becoming a new creature, and walking in purpose there is a reintroduction that needs to happen. I can no longer associate myself with brokenness, past behaviors, and "Little Ole Nia" that some claim me to be. Due to history that some may have, the history of "Little Ole Nia" may outweigh the version of me that represents God. I know that everything I experience, is recorded in the Bible, so I want to give an example of Jesus needing to be reintroduced:

To paraphrase, In Mark 6: 2-4, While teaching one day, Jesus was scorned at because the people He was teaching had close relationship to Him, and knew His personal life, such as his former occupation, which was being a carpenter, and his siblings. Because of knowing these details, the people discredited His teaching. Interestingly, there are times when people know your past, or present, and can discredit who you are, or who you will become because of their knowledge of personal details, and former experiences.

In my life, the "reintroduction" phase has been, and still can be a struggle. Some people may associate me with still being the future nurse that I always dreamed of, or the relative that may be living the average teenage lifestyle—which is not true. I believe there can be a struggle when some may not understand the growth, new direction, and God's hand that is present in my life. Some may not understand my deep relationship with God, one that goes beyond surface level and that causes God to be in the center of it all. God orders my steps, gives me wisdom, and is the one whom I submit to. In Mark 6, we see that amongst the people that have close relationships with Jesus can still reside relationships that hold very little honor to Him.

I believe that in this honorable transition that I have made at an early age—which is to walk in God's plan for my life, relationships who care for me should honor my decision and respect the new becoming of me. I have had to do a lot of reintroducing who I have become. But mostly, I have had to remind myself of who I am and who I am not. I knew the old Nia for so long, when she was broken, confused, and in need of healing—the Nia that aspired nursing, and other occupations that God did not intend. Many times, I had to go back to God's promises and align my wants with his plans. It wasn't and isn't easy, but it is a constant process of surrender and submission.

Though the old me was gone and I was brand new, I was still the same Nia. I was simply conforming to God's best version of me. Cheesecake Factory is still my favorite restaurant, and Mac cosmetics was still my go to, but my heart and mind were set on higher altitudes for God. With God's transformation in me, I became whole, and full of God's freedom—certainly a new Nia. Reintroducing myself to family, friends, and colleagues was essential… but I also had to reintroduce myself to the enemy and his demons. I was now a redeemed daughter of the Most High. The enemy had no chains over me and I wanted him to know that I was stronger than ever. I was determined to keep myself and the generations after me—free. Any seeds within my lineage would rot and be completely removed with the power and grace of God through my reintroduction. My obedience towards God was exactly what my lineage needed for a new beginning.

My entrance to the world was out of wedlock and brought feelings of abandonment, but as time prospered, I began to understand the generational curses upon me. To give reference to generational curses in the Bible, when we read Deuteronomy 28 we find valuable information:

To paraphrase Deuteronomy 28:1-14, God is promising the Israelites that if the Israelites remain obedient, they will receive blessings from God. Specifically verse 4 states that their children will be blessed if they remain obedient. In other words, generational blessings are, and can be a result of obedience. Then in Deuteronomy 28: 15-18, God, in the next verses, is very clear that there are consequences if the Israelites do not remain obedient. Verse 18 specifically states that their children will be cursed. Through this passage in Deuteronomy we see the context to the meaning of blessings and curses, and that the obedience of one can contribute to generational blessings or curses. There are other stories in the Bible, such as David's, who was a king but was lustful, and therefore perverse issues that resulted in his son to have sexual relations with his other child.

As generational blessings and curses are tied to one's obedience, I believe it is important to understand that the enemy wants families to pass down curses rather than blessings. John 10:10 says, "The enemy comes to steal, kill and destroy, but I (Jesus), come that they may have life, and life more abundantly." The enemies plan is to steal, kill, and destroy the plans God has for us, and through curses, we are bound to live according to the enemies plan. Because I have chosen to be obedient, my obedience will result in blessings for me, but also for generations after me. The spirit of abandonment that rested heavily in my life, and other spirits such as lust, which resulted in me being born out of wedlock, can no longer exist—as I have been set free, I will, and generations will be free indeed. There is a reintroduction of myself to the enemy, he cannot reign on my bloodline anymore. Through my redemption, and obedience to God, I believe that the fruit of my womb will be blessed. Together, me and my future husband will set a firm foundation, and together break generational curses. With this reintroduction to the ones closest to me, and even to darkness I continue to become the woman of God that walks in my calling and virtue.

CHAPTER 10 - Conclusion: Becoming

"He has saved us and called us to a holy life--not because of anything we have done but because of his own purpose and grace. This grace was given to us in Christ Jesus before the beginning of time."

(2 Timothy 1:9 NIV)

With matriculation, at some point we become something in life. The good, or the bad experiences, work together to bring us to some expected end. Looking at a butterfly, this beautiful insect does not automatically at birth have the wings, or colors it has further in its matriculation. There is a change that happens, or metaphoric as a scientist would say, that contributes to the adult stage being different from the first stage, as being an egg.

First, the butterfly starts off as an egg, in my life, I would associate this moment to before I was born, but I was in my mother's womb. The next stage of a butterfly is the caterpillar, which is referred to as the feeding stage. In my life, I absorbed a lot. Not being exempt from the circumstances, and issues of life, what I absorbed may have not been the "healthiest" but thankfully, I had a transition stage. The transition stage is the third stage of a butterfly, as there are inward changes that will soon be expressed on the outside. God had to do an inside work to ensure I would be able to express Him on the outside, or in other works including writing this book. The fourth stage of the butterfly, is the adult stage, also known as the reproductive stages. The adult stage is the final stage of the butterfly, and the butterfly reaches its final purpose, which is to reproduce.

In life, there are stages that will lead us into becoming something. As you are reading this, maybe you feel as if the "feeding stage" of your life resulted in you absorbing things you never thought you would, or things that may still be on the inside right now. I want you to know that there is a transition season where you can lay all of your burdens down and find rest in God, the One who created You, and even knows the amount of hairs on your head. Transitioning is always made available, and in the transition, you begin to become who God first intended you to be. In the moment of my transition, I knew that I was moving closer to God than I ever experienced, but I really did not know what was on the other side of becoming closer to Him. I never knew that I would be ministering, or even writing this book to tell my story, and inspire people to let go of experiences that were beyond their control and surrender to God withholding nothing. Even in the midst of not knowing what God had, and still has for my life—He knew. He knew that the plans He has for me would blow my mind, and that I would experience peace, and one day be a mouthpiece on Earth for Him.

I'm not the only one that can experience becoming the "butterfly" or who God first intended His people to be. In the book of Jeremiah, God told Jeremiah that before he was formed in his mother's womb he was called to become something, and to be used by God. In the same way, before we were born God has called us to become the versions of ourselves that He first intended. While reading this, I hope there has been a seed planted to desire to be redeemed and become the very person God has destined you to be.

For too long we can be bound, and never experience the life God has intended. It is through forsaking our past, surrenderance, and becoming wholeheartedly devoted to our Creator that we experience the purpose in which He created us.

Prayer

Father in the name of Jesus, it is a desire to see You glorified in this book. I pray that every reader will come into alignment with who You have called them to be. I come against the hinderances of sin, being bound because of past experiences, and the darkness that has not allowed them to see the Light — which is You. I declare that every reader will yield their lives to You, the One True Savior, and be redeemed to become who You have called them to be. In Jesus Name, Amen.

ABOUT THE AUTHOR

In recent years, Nia Robinson entered into the intercessory prayer ministry and accepted her called to preach publicly in December 2019. She has a strong passion for women to shake off their brokenness, and enter into the wholeness that only God can bring. She exemplifies being the woman God has called her to be with this scripture dear to her heart: Proverbs 31:30 — «Charm is deceitful and beauty is fleeting but awoman who fears the Lord, shall be praised!»

In her debut book, "She Knows: Once Bound But Now Redeemed To Become," she puts an emphasis on the fact that the bound can be redeemed through God and become who He has called them to be.

www.ingramcontent.com/pod-product-compliance
Lightning Source LLC
Chambersburg PA
CBHW070951180426
43194CB00041B/2046